MW00712579

The Flower of Arnold

John A. Ward

Published by

Dayglo Books Ltd, Nottingham, UK

www.dayglobooks.co.uk

0006-14-1025-13

© John A. Ward 2014

The right of John A. Ward to be identified as the author
of this work has been asserted by him in accordance
with the Designs and Copyright Act 1988.

Cover artwork & illustrations by
www.valentineart.co.uk

Typeset in Opendyslexic
by Abelardo Gonzales (2013)

Printed by IngramSpark

Distributed by Filament Publishing Ltd, Croydon

This book is subject to international copyright and may
not be copied in any way without the prior written
permission of the publishers.

Foreword

By Mrs Edna Hindle, former Mayor of Gedling Borough Council, 1993.

I was extremely pleased when I heard that a book was to be produced to commemorate HMS Pennywort – and of the efforts made by the people of Arnold to raise the money to purchase that ship during the long, dark days of World War Two.

I was shown a photograph of the crew of HMS Pennywort who came to the offices of the Arnold Urban District Council to celebrate the adoption of their ship in March 1942 and were given a special plaque to commemorate this event.

I enquired where the plaque was to be found, but the Council had disposed of it when refurbishing the offices.

I learned that, fortunately, a dedicated supporter of the Royal Navy had taken it to the Royal Naval Club in Nottingham.

During my year in office as Mayor, the 50th anniversary of the Battle of the Atlantic was being celebrated and the custodian of the plaque kindly allowed it to be restored to its rightful place.

I invited the surviving members of the crew of HMS Pennywort to a special occasion at the Civic Centre in Arnot Hill Park where the plaque now hangs, and I am delighted to say that many attended.

Every Remembrance Sunday, the Royal British Legion and members of youth organisations parade from St Paul's church to the War Memorial on Arnot Hill Park for a Remembrance Service.

The Service is followed by the placing of a wreath by the Mayor on the plaque to HMS Pennywort, as the plaque is now recognised as an official War Memorial.

We must never forget the service given, and the price paid, by the men of the Royal and Merchant Navies during the war. We especially like to remember Arnold's own warship HMS Pennywort which also played a part in Operation Overlord, the Normandy landings.

Edna Hindle

Introduction

At 11.30am on Saturday 28th May 1993, a group of fifteen men came from all over the country to gather at the Arnold Civic Centre at Arnot Hill Park, Nottingham. They came to share a common bond.

They were all ex-sailors of HMS Pennywort – a 'Flower Class' corvette which had been adopted by the people of Arnold.

The men were the known survivors of HMS Pennywort's crew under their Commanding Officer Lt. G.C.W. Meldrum RNR, to become Captain MN, RTD, MBE.

Shipmate Denyer from Southampton
Shipmate Erridge from Eastbourne
Shipmate Guest from Warrington
Shipmate Hill from Stourbridge
Shipmate J. E. Jones from Ruthin
Shipmate S. Jones from Surbiton
Shipmate Holder from Minehead

Shipmate Lynch from Liverpool

Shipmate Lyon from Birmingham

Shipmate Mitchell from Carlisle

Shipmate O'Sullivan from Beaconsfield

Shipmate Oxenbury from Bradpole

Shipmate Sparkes from Cardiff

Shipmate Stephens from Cirencester

Shipmate Ward from London

Since these men assembled at Arnold in 1993 their numbers have dwindled further.

I had difficulty contacting some of the men, for a variety of reasons. Some are still reluctant to talk about the terrible experiences they suffered during the war years.

I respect their sentiments and pay tribute to the many men of many nations, both Merchant and Royal Navies, who were involved in the North Atlantic convoys – a great number of whom were never to return.

Some of them were little more than just boys at that time. Memories may dim, but they will always be remembered.

John A. Ward

The Flower of Arnold

Chapter 1 – Setting the Scene

Following the introductions at the re-dedication ceremony on 28th May 1993 by the Mayor of Gedling, a response and a short talk were given by Sub. Lt. Stan Jones. He told of the last great convoy during the Battle of the Atlantic in March 1943, when more than forty U-boats struck.

During the battle, dozens of Dutchmen and Norwegians were rescued from the sea, following the sinking of their ships by U-boat torpedoes.

Stan Jones went on to tell how the crew of HMS Pennywort ferried British troops to the beaches of Normandy on D-Day, 6th June 1944 – quite a long time after the convoys.

Perhaps the most poignant moment of the whole occasion was four lines read from a poem, written and read by Larry Lynch, a Pennywort crew member who recorded the exploits of his ship at the time in verse:

"That stout corvette sails proudly on
A ship without a care.
When duty calls, without a doubt
Pennywort shall be there!"

The Nottingham Evening Post reported the reunion, and what an emotional occasion it was for the crew members to meet again.

The Flower Class Corvette Association has around seven hundred veterans in Full Membership worldwide, with another three hundred or more family members as Associates.

Sadly, the numbers continue to reduce, reflecting the age of these ex-sailors – men still strongly bonded together after so many years by their shared war time experiences.

Chapter 2 – What was HMS Pennywort?

A look into a book about wild flowers will reveal the following:

"The Pennywort derives its name from the small, penny-like leaves. It is found in abundance in marshy areas throughout England. It has tiny clusters of green-white flowers on short stalks. It is a creeping plant found growing on moss, but sometimes floating freely on water."

This is not a very exciting description for a British warship, but considering that almost three hundred Flower Class corvettes were built during the war, I expect it became progressively harder to find names for them.

However, the part of the description: "floating freely on water" was appropriate, because HMS Pennywort saved hundreds of shipwrecked survivors from the icy waters of the North Atlantic.

The design of the Flower Class corvettes was based on the whale catcher "Southern Pride", a ship built in 1936 for the Southern Whaling and Sealing Company of Cape Town, South Africa and later purchased by the Royal Navy.

Southern Pride was lost after running aground near Monrovia, West Africa, in June 1944.

The Flower Class corvettes were built specifically for the protection of coastal convoys, but very early in the war they were used as ocean escorts.

HMS Pennywort was built on Clydeside and launched on 18th October 1941.

The construction time was 11 months and 22 days – quite an achievement for such a project!

The total cost of the vessel was ninety thousand pounds.

HMS Pennywort was oil-powered. She was fitted with a standard 4-cylinder triple-expansion reciprocating engine with a single propeller, and was capable of a maximum speed of 16 knots. Her full-speed range was about 2,600 miles – or 3,450 miles at 12 knots.

She displaced 950 tons – about a quarter the size of a modern cross-channel ferry – and 1,160 tons fully laden. She was 205 feet in length with a beam of 32 feet. Her bunkers held 230 tons of fuel oil.

She carried a ship's company of 80 men.

The captains of the Royal Navy Flower Class corvettes mostly came from the Merchant Navy, and the officers and crew from the Royal Navy Reserve (RNR) or Royal Navy Voluntary Reserve (RNVR).

HMS Pennywort's first captain was Lt. G.C.W. Meldrum RNR. The crew joined the vessel on 20th February 1942. After taking on fuel, stores and supplies the ship took part in trials off the coast of Ireland for two weeks.

After that, she went to Tobermory in Scotland, the Royal Navy Training Base for escort duties. The trials had been successful and she was assigned to Escort Group B4, based at Londonderry in Northern Ireland.

One main difference between HMS Pennywort and other corvettes was the addition of an "acoustic hammer" fitted to the bows to destroy mines.

This was a strange device, comprising an 'A' bracket protruding from the bows, which had a large bucket attached that could be raised or lowered.

The bucket was lowered into the sea and a heavy weight dropped into it. The idea was that the sound created in this way would ripple out and detonate any acoustic mines in the immediate area.

She was also fitted with routine mine-sweeping gear.

HMS Pennywort was ready for duty. She carried the pennant number K.111 and the motto of the Flower Class Corvette Association: "Without haste but unresting."

Chapter 3 – Fundraising

Having met one of the many warships so urgently needed in the war effort, let us look at how the residents of Arnold became involved.

The 17th to the 24th May 1941 was declared "War Weapons Week" and the people of Great Britain were urged by the government to raise £50,000 for the purpose of buying ten fighter planes.

To raise £50,000 in 1941 was really quite a lot to ask. The average wage was only around £6 a week.

The money was not to be a donation, but a loan. As the Nottingham Advertiser for 10th May 1941 put it:

"All that is wanted is for everybody to lend – and lend so freely that it becomes really a sacrifice."

Everyone was encouraged to do their bit and support a range of social activities that had been organised to run during that week.

The landed gentry and Members of Parliament were present at the grand opening ceremony. There were speeches, and a parade of members of the military services with war-time equipment headed by a band.

In the evening there was a concert, and next day a grand church parade involving Special Constables, the Home Guard, the British Legion, Air Raid Patrol services, the Army Fire Service, the Red Cross and St John's Ambulance brigade. Once again, a military band was in attendance.

They played again on Monday at a big sports event. The principle attraction was a knockout football tournament between the various services that had paraded the previous day.

There was a girls' hockey match, and the ladies of the Control Room went up against the First Aid Ladies in a tug-of-war tournament.

Meanwhile, the messenger boys of the Air Raid Patrol took on the police messenger boys in a bicycle polo match.

On Tuesday there was a whist drive and dance, with another whist drive on Wednesday. There was a performance by The Blackout Concert Party on Thursday, and on Friday there were full-scale Air Raid Patrol exercises throughout the district.

Saturday afternoon was given over to displays of dancing and physical training, concluding in the evening with a dance on the lawn at Arnot Hill Park.

To us today, the events don't appear all that exciting, but the public were under an awful lot of restrictions during wartime, so any organised leisure activities were very welcome.

At the start of War Weapons Week it was reported that £50,000 was regarded as a modest sum to raise and was "really, far too low."

After all, as the newspaper pointed out, the money to be raised was a loan – not given. The public were urged to invest their cash because the government would pay interest. Money in National Savings could be withdrawn easily.

"That is not too much to ask of anyone at this vital time," the editorial thundered, "when the most stern struggle in the nation's history is taking place."

Indicator boards were set up at strategic points along main streets to show the daily totals raised.

The people of Arnold, and the surrounding district, pulled out all the stops.

At the end of the third day £49,647 had already been subscribed – only £353 below the target.

Chapter 4 – Warship Week

Following the success of War Weapons Week, and the increase in hostilities in the war, the need for more ships was quickly recognised.

The value of the convoy system was huge, and became of paramount importance for the protection of vital supplies to and from Britain.

It was with this in mind that the British government announced "Warship Week".

Towns and villages throughout the nation were urged to save money to buy escort ships. Arnold was again to step up to the challenge, and a committee was formed to plan Warship Week.

The residents of the seven local boroughs joined forces to try to raise £120,000 to finance the cost of a corvette for the Royal Navy.

Arnold's Warship Week was fixed for 21st – 28th May 1942, and the name of the warship was HMS Pennywort.

Once again, the 'need for sacrifice' and the aim of the appeal made the press. It quoted the ship's Commanding Officer, three months after he took over the newly built ship:

"We of HMS Pennywort have learnt with great pleasure and deep gratitude of our proposed 'adoption' by you. Thanking you all and wishing every success to your war effort. Lt G.C.W. Meldrum RNR."

The fundraising began modestly enough with £13 raised at a whist drive, but by the end of the campaign a staggering £170,000 had been subscribed.

Street 'savings groups' were formed and their hard-working organisers went from house to house, collecting money from the occupants.

Mrs Mead and her helpers toiled up and down the steep slope of Breckhill Road to visit 116 houses who, between them, donated £1,107 – amounting to almost £10 from each house.

The tin-rattling on Thackeray's Lane brought in a further £1,419, but they were outdone by the group on Whernside Road who came back with £2,073.

Mrs Hampson, leading the Marlborough Road group, persuaded the 32 homes she called on to hand over £150 each, bringing in a total of £4,800.

But the undisputed champion was Mrs Day on Buckingham Road who raised a total of £6,175 from 29 houses.

Probably the most unusual stunt to raise money was the re-enactment of a stagecoach robbery on Arnot Hill Road by a man dressed as Dick Turpin.

Children took part in fundraising too. The pupils of Hilwyn Preparatory School, whose ages ranged from 4 to 11, had been saving up since October and were able to donate £36 for a rubber dinghy and £40 for a parachute.

In addition to that magnificent effort, they invested £144 during Warship Week.

The children were very devoted to helping the war effort. They also adopted the crew of a tank and arranged to keep them supplied with knitted comforts, cigarettes, chocolates and magazines.

Many of the children's fathers would have been away from home serving in the Army, the Navy or the Air Force, so although the children were very young, the situation was very real to them.

During 1942, the crew of HMS Pennywort visited Arnold and took part in an Adoption Ceremony, following which they went to the library to visit local ladies who were packing up medical supplies.

The usual parades and social entertainments were laid on to encourage people to become involved in the campaign.

This time there was also a boxing tournament and a Naval exhibition, spotlighting the Navy's activities and weapons.

There were rousing words quoted in the press from Admiral "Teddy" Evans, First World War hero and Antarctic explorer:

"I send you my best wishes for the launching of Arnold's Warship Week. I believe that war savings aimed at the right target soon amount to a warship.

"Gallantry and good sense demand all-in savings efforts for those whose duties and devotions are always concerned with saving us.

"I hope Arnold will fire its broadside for the Royal Navy and thereby assist to blow the enemy out of the war!"

The actual cost of HMS Pennywort was:

Hull	£ 55,000
Main and auxiliary machinery	£50,000
Armament and ammunition	£13,500
Motor boats, anchors, cables, etc	£1,500
Total cost	£120,000

Chapter 5 – The Convoys

As we've already seen, when she had completed successful sea trials, HMS Pennywort was assigned to B4 Escort Group based at Londonderry.

HMS Pennywort – known to her crew as "The Tiddly P" – escorted several convoys which proved to be fairly uneventful until, unfortunately, she ran aground on her way into harbour at Newfoundland.

She sustained severe damage and had to be towed to Halifax, Nova Scotia. She was sent to Boston, Massachusetts for repairs and then returned to Halifax at the very time when the Germans started unprecedented attacks on Allied convoys.

She stood by the "Robert Colly", which broke in half in heavy weather and, together with another Flower Class corvette, HMS Borage, rescued her crew.

Later, the two 'flowers' again combined their efforts and stood by the "Empire Tarpo", which had engine trouble.

The vessels of B4 Escort Group began their duties escorting convoys across the Atlantic during October and November.

By the following March they were deployed to escort one hundred and sixty merchant vessels out of New York and Newfoundland, bound for the UK.

Great Britain was hard pressed to produce all the food it needed during wartime. Food and other items were strictly rationed. The country depended on supplies from across the Atlantic, however perilous the journey.

Sixty-four ships were formed into the first convoy, carrying general cargo as well as military stores, oil seed, wheat, steel, soya, timber and explosives. The convoy was escorted by five Flower Class corvettes, a destroyer, a frigate, a trawler and a US Coastguard cutter.

However, the German navy deployed forty-six U-boats to intercept the convoy, and despite the best efforts of the escort vessels, eight of the sixty-four cargo ships were sunk.

Meanwhile, HMS Pennywort was on duty escorting the second convoy, along with seven destroyers and three more Flower Class corvettes. They were guarding some forty vessels transporting meat, butter, cheese, manganese, steel, cotton, animal feed, grain, fuel oil, wheat, zinc, sugar and powdered milk.

Such was the ferocity and precision of the Germany U-boat attack, however, they were unable to prevent the loss of thirteen of their merchant ships.

A further nine ships from the third convoy were lost on their way over to England.

HMS Pennywort picked up 127 survivors from the water. These men, plus those rescued by other escort ships, were landed at Greenock, in Scotland.

The U-boats caused havoc and carnage in the North Atlantic during those difficult times, but they also encountered death and destruction at sea. Twelve U-boats were known to have been sunk.

Each U-boat would have carried a crew of approximately fifty. Of these six hundred men, only forty-one survived.

Chapter 6 – Operation Overlord

HMS Pennywort continued to escort convoys between May and October 1943.

Whilst accompanying one convoy on 18th October, she stood by the merchant ship "Blair Devon" and then on the 20th she stood by the "Begum" which had lost a propeller.

Eventually, the "Tiddly P" reached Gibraltar on 1st November 1943. Her next stop was the Tyne, where she was sent for repairs, which took several months to complete.

The code name for the Normandy Landings was Operation Overlord. The naval part of the campaign was known as Operation Neptune.

By the time HMS Pennywort's repairs were done, preparations for Operation Neptune were well advanced. It was clear that huge resources would be required and HMS Pennywort would be one of the vessels involved.

On D-Day plus one – June 7th – HMS Pennywort began escort duty to the Normandy beachhead.

The real horror of those days is captured in a letter written many years later by a man named Ernest Cheetham, who had read a newspaper article about a Polish cruiser, "Dragon", which took part in the D-Day landings. He wrote to the paper as follows:

"I was involved in recovering one of the sailors who lost his life on the cruiser.

"Being in the Royal Navy, our Craft Recovery Unit had twenty-one men on Mike Red Beach.

"I was 19. Our Commanding Officer instructed myself and a comrade to go out to the "Dragon" to recover the sailor's body, which was trapped under some pipes in the engine room.

"My job was to cut through the pipes with gas-burning equipment, which I did. His head, one arm and a leg was missing, but I clearly remember he still had his identity disc around his neck.

"I don't know what happened after recovering the sailor. I was told that the cruiser had been struck by a one-man torpedo."

What Ernest Cheetham did not know was that twenty-six sailors were lost in that torpedo attack.

The "Dragon" was finally towed inshore to the Mulberry harbour and sunk, as part of the artificial breakwater. HMS Pennywort assisted in that operation.

Following Ernest Cheetham's letter to the paper, he was interviewed by a reporter and gave a striking, first-hand account of what it was like to be there.

He landed at midday on D-Day and spent nearly three months on the beaches of Normandy with his Craft Recovery Unit, watching the sea turn red as bombing raids helped turn the course of the war.

Soon after landing on Juno Beach, Ernest Cheetham was sent out to check a small landing craft.

"I went out and found that it had been badly damaged. I got on board and opened the doors, and behind them was the most handsome looking lad with black wavy hair. But his face was white as a sheet, he was obviously dead. It makes you sick – the lad was only probably 18 or 19."

That was the same age as Ernest himself, a fresh-faced commando who joined up less than a year before, on August 17th 1943. A joiner by trade, experienced in welding and riveting, he was assigned to one of the Craft Recovery Units.

From the moment they left the south coast in the early hours of June 6th 1944, there were many terrible sights – and little in the way of light relief.

"Before setting off we were told to write letters to our next of kin as we would be very lucky to get back," he said. "Our job was to get the damaged landing craft up on the beach and repair what we could.

"We landed about midnight on Juno Beach and I remember the crossing was awful. We set off from Southampton and travelled overnight.

"Alongside us was another vessel, and when you looked across, some of them were vertical with the waves. I'm pretty certain I was the last one to get seasick out of my crew, but we all did.

"I had a hammock near the drive shafts and the smell of diesel oil got to me. I couldn't get off quick enough. When we landed, the tide was well up, but when it went out there were arms, legs and bodies lying everywhere.

"Two days after landing there were bodies all over the beach – sixty, seventy, eighty, all young lads and all dead. The sea was red. When you saw all the dead bodies as the tide went out, it was just a terrible sight.

"We were terrified. You've got to dig yourself in and there are guns going off left, right and centre. Aircraft firing at you and buzz bombs that we used to try and shoot down. It's an experience which is truly frightening – anybody that says they're not afraid, that's lies. They were, and I was, but we got through it, thank God.

"When we landed, we were sprayed with machine gun fire from the Germans in "pill boxes".

"The Canadians, who I have the greatest respect for, went in first. There was a pill box there and a German came out surrendering after having sprayed the lot of us. It didn't help him. He got sprayed over the pill box with a bayonet.

"Once on the beach, we had to dig ourselves in and protect ourselves against constant attacks.

"I had to dig a hole on the beach – it was like digging a grave six foot deep – and two of us slept in it the first night, before we made proper "fox holes". They had armour plates on either side and over the top, and sand bags on top of that. We lived in them for the whole length of time we were there – about two or three months.

"When we were in them it looked like the tracer fire was coming straight at us.

"One of the most frightening experiences for me was the Germans firing eleven-inch shells from a gun every night. A hell of a lot of damage was done and it was a great relief when the beach commander came round and told us, 'You can forget Big Bertha because we've got in and blasted it.'

"I had to do a repair one day. A part had come off a crane and I was sent up to fix it. Something nearly hit me and I said, 'Stop bloody throwing things!'

"But it was a sniper firing at me. I jumped off there, a twenty-foot drop into the sand! The Petty Officer told me to get up behind the beach where it was safe, but I was still there digging in the sand, afraid.

"I saw the whole of a huge air raid. There must have been at least a thousand bombers going over to drop their bombs. It was a tremendous sight.

"Every day there were bombers coming over – our lads – all day long, bombing the hell out of them. I saw two planes fall during that raid, and one or two parachutes coming down.

"You wonder how they made it through the flak.

"Throughout it all, we only lost one of our guys. I made the coffin bottom for his burial. When we went to bury him, a machine gun started firing and only two of us remained standing, me and the padre. We were there armed with just a .38 revolver.

"There was one thing that brought a smile to my face. We went out to this barge, this old looking thing which had been covered up for days. We stopped to look over the side of it and found a wooden box full of medical supplies, including rum!

"There was twenty-one gallons of it, and it made sure that we got to sleep pretty easy that night!"

Chapter 7 – HMS Pennywort's Final Duties

Following HMS Pennywort's successful duties at the Normandy Landings she returned to Grimsby from the 16th to 28th July 1944 for repairs and then took up her duties with the Portsmouth Patrol.

Early September saw her sailing for the Clyde. Her duties were quite mundane, following all the activity of the past convoys and her involvement at Normandy.

She became the weather reporting ship for the North Atlantic and performed two such duties until November. December saw her revert back to convoy duties, working out of Liverpool.

In January 1945 she escorted the merchant ship "Henry Miller" into Gibraltar. From there she returned to Tobermory and eventually back to Londonderry, where she was laid up in reserve.

In February 1949 she was towed to Troon for

break up, always a sad end for any ship. It was also the sad end of a historic connection with Arnold.

During the whole of her commissioned time with the fleet, HMS Pennywort never lost a man through enemy action.

One man was lost overboard during a refuelling operation at sea.

From what I have been told by some of the men who sailed in her, she was a happy ship, which proved to be an efficient fighting unit of the Escort Groups during World War Two.

The men of HMS Pennywort had to endure many hazards, as all men at sea experienced, but in their case many added dangers confronted them during the days of the North Atlantic convoys.

Bearing in mind the vital work they were involved in, escorting badly needed supplies of food and war materials, the men of the convoys never flinched from their duties.

They were well aware of the constant threat from the sea and from the enemy. The North Atlantic was a hostile place at the best of times during the war, and in the winter months even more so.

If a man was unlucky enough to be ditched into the sea for whatever reason, rescue was almost impossible. The man would freeze to death in minutes.

Germany was hell-bent on interrupting and sinking as many convoy ships as possible. Admiral Karl Donitz concentrated large numbers of U-boats (the "wolf packs") to hunt and destroy the convoys.

More problems were caused by the thick ice which formed on the rigging and vital equipment on board, making working and even walking on the decks extra difficult.

Added to this, there was yet another constant threat. Almost all the aircraft of Coastal Command were incapable of long distance sea patrol and the crews had no training in anti-submarine operations.

The planes were equipped with a bomb that had to fall within six to eight feet of a submarine to cause it serious damage. The trouble was, these bombs tended to bounce back before exploding, becoming more of a threat than the U-boats.

The area that the long range aircraft could not cover was known as the "Air Gap" or, to the Germans, "The Black Pit".

In 1942, after the initial activities of the German U-boats, the offensive began to wane a little. Four hundred and fifty ships in nineteen convoys reached the British Isles in March 1942 without any losses.

Admiral Donitz had switched the main concentration of his U-boats to the east of the United States, but he became so frustrated by the U.S. convoys, with their air cover and surface escorts, that he decided to return to the Atlantic.

In the autumn of 1942 Admiral Donitz had so many U-boats that he permitted the "wolf packs" to attack shipping whenever the opportunity arose, either submerged by day, or on the surface at night.

Shipping losses reached a peak in November 1942. One hundred and seventeen ships, amounting to over seven hundred thousand tons, were sunk by the U-boats.

Germany was building U-boats faster than the building of the escort vessels here in Britain. The corvettes had been hastily built and were intended for use as coastal escorts but, as we have seen, they were required to carry out ocean escort duties.

These darkest days of the North Atlantic convoys took a terrible toll on men, ships and supplies.

By late April 1943 an average of one hundred and eight U-boats were operating in, or close to, the Air Gap.

Thirty-seven outward and homeward bound merchant ships were sunk that month.

Escort vessels and aircraft, working together, went on the attack and managed to sink nearly thirty U-boats, so during May there was a decline in the attacks and sinkings.

Rear Admiral W.S. Chalmers wrote:

"The enemy feared the combined onslaught of the sea and air forces and could not stand up to their numbers, equipment, endurance and skill.

"The spirit of the enemy was broken by the steadfast resistance of the crews of the merchant ships, which outshone in courage and tenacity any siege in history."

The lives of the men of HMS Pennywort were exposed to danger from many angles, yet these brave souls went to sea time after time without complaint, knowing they were serving their country to the best of their ability.

They were praised in a newspaper article printed just after D-Day:

"When HMS Pennywort – a ship that has the reputation of always being at the right spot – rescued the entire crew of a Dutch ship, the crew presented it with three silver cups and a Dutch flag.

"The Dutchmen were some of the scores who have been saved from the sea by HMS Pennywort in the North Atlantic and off the Normandy beaches.

"Some of the survivors were severely wounded. A 19-year-old Sick Berth Attendant, handling broken legs like an expert, was congratulated on his work by the doctor who came on board later."

A former crew member, Sid Oxenbury, who joined the Navy aged 17, and sailed on HMS Pennywort, passed on some recollections of the D-Day landings:

"On Monday, June 5th, extra ammunition and stores were loaded, and the Pennywort set sail early on June 6th for Normandy. In her role as escort, she kept watch for German E-boats and U-boats as the invasion fleet of six-and-a-half-thousand vessels made its way across the Channel.

"We had an inkling what was happening beforehand because of what we were doing.

"When we got to Portsmouth we saw masses of landing craft being prepared. There were soldiers there, all along the coast, getting ready. There were lots of Americans there.

"It wasn't until setting sail that the crew was told by the captain what was happening. He told us to expect seventy percent casualties.

"HMS Pennywort remained on constant watch as it sailed up and down the Normandy coastline, protecting ships that were anchored and engaged in bombardment. These included the battleship "Rodney", firing twenty miles inland at a Germany armoured column approaching the coast.

"During a short break from the firing, Pennywort was able to go alongside the "Rodney" to receive a ton of potatoes, as the ship had run out of food except for dehydrated stock.

"I will never forget the bravery of the nurses I saw clambering down into the sea from a large hospital ship as large as a liner. They were shoulder-deep in sea water as they made for the beach to tend the wounded. They did a terrific job. When we saw them, a big cheer went up from our ship. They never thought about the danger. They were about the same age as me – I'll never forget that.

"One of my lasting memories is pulling survivors on to the ship. We rescued a number of men, including the crew of a tanker who were engulfed in thick, black oil. The main problem was getting them up the scrambling nets – if they'd had a leg blown off or something it was very difficult pulling them up.

"The tanker survivors were taken to Portsmouth. Pennywort spent about six weeks up and down the Normandy coastline. It was a mission fraught with danger. What appeared to be a body in the sea – with battledress and helmet – could have been a German ruse and contained a sea mine. If you touched it, you'd be dead.

"Early on, we were under attack because all the enemy guns were ready for us. We were lucky. Other ships were sunk. I've always thought how lucky we were as a ship. We were mobile all the time so we stood a better chance.

"I was the only signalman, but once we got there, all the forces worked together – we had to do it, there was no going back. We had to beat them so we could get inland and do the job. We were one ship out of masses of other ships doing the same thing. We just got on with it."

HMS Pennywort was a happy and efficient ship that is remembered with pride. Every man knew his duty and carried it out unflinchingly. The men were teammates and friends, dependent upon each other, which made them efficient – and that showed through thousands of times during the war, both on land and at sea.

Chapter 8 – The Poems

Many men joined up in their teens. Some volunteered, not waiting for the inevitable call up.

Today, it's all but impossible to imagine how they coped with the terrible dangers they were thrust into. They had to grow up fast and learn to face death and terrible injuries, on a daily basis.

Some crew members have never found it possible to speak about what they saw during the war, finding it too painful bringing to mind the horrors of those experiences.

Others have put their deepest thoughts and feelings into words in the form of poems.

A.J. Davies, dwelling on his memories, wrote:

"How can I express,
How can I tell,
In these days of peace,
Of the days that were hell?"

A.J. Davies was a stoker on board HMS Pennywort.

His description of the ship being attacked by a depth charge, while he was working below the water line, is chilling indeed:

"A mighty blast, the lights go dim
Our stern lifts from the sea,
Explosives numb my senses
And life stands still for me.

When the bell rings the danger's past
And safe the convoy keep.
Just think of this young stoker,
Who served beneath the deep.

Also think, we are locked down
Below the ocean's swell,
Going about our stoking
With a fear that made our hell.

I know it's true, I served my time
In stoke-hold way down deep,
Yet still today, I say those words –
Pray God my soul to keep."

Larry Lynch wrote a poem to celebrate the many rescues that HMS Pennywort carried out:

"The Pennywort steamed slowly round,
All danger scorned with hate.
Men were to be rescued quickly,
Or else 'twould be too late.

Soon duty called, a cruiser hit
Was signalling for aid,
Quickly "P" was on the spot,
The distance swiftly made.

The sturdy cruiser did not sink
Although her stern was low,
And soon the saviour Pennywort
Had taken her in tow.

Another merchant ship went down,
Her crew swam valiantly,
And Pennywort was there again
To save them from the sea.

That corvette stout sails proudly on,
A ship without a care,
When duty calls, without a doubt,
Pennywort shall be there!"

I will leave it to the 17th century poet, Thomas
Traherne, to have the final word on courage:

"Strange is the vigour in a brave man's soul.

The strength of his spirit and his irresistible power,

The greatness of his heart and the height of his
condition,

His mighty confidence and his contempt of dangers,

His true security and repose in himself,

His liberty to dare and to do what he pleaseth,

His alacrity in the midst of fears,

His invincible temper,

Are advantages which make him master of fortune.

His courage fits him for all attempts,

Makes him serviceable to God and man,

And makes him the bulwark and defence,

Of his being and his country."

This is an extract from a longer, illustrated book entitled "The Flower of Arnold – The Story of Arnold's Adopted Warship" published by John A. Ward in 2004

Sunset Lady

A tale from

Operation Dynamo –

the Evacuation of the

Dunkirk Beaches

26th May to 4th June 1940

Published by

Dayglo Books Ltd, Nottingham, UK

www.dayglobooks.co.uk

0006-14-1225-13

© Philip Baker 2014

The right of Philip Baker to be identified as the author
of this work has been asserted by him in accordance
with the Designs and Copyright Act 1988.

Cover artwork & illustrations by
www.valentineart.co.uk

Typeset in Opendyslexic
by Abelardo Gonzales (2013)

Printed by IngramSpark

Distributed by Filament Publishing Ltd, Croydon

This book is subject to international copyright and may
not be copied in any way without the prior written
permission of the publishers.

Sunset Lady

Chapter 1 – One Little Ship

I think it is fair to say our little town of Burroport was always proud of Sunset Lady and the notable part she played in the evacuation of our troops from the beaches of Dunkirk, in May 1940.

I knew her well, having been around the harbour since childhood. She was built for the Royal Navy in 1918 as a 32-foot motor cutter and sold, unused, as 'government surplus', to a man named James Thorpe.

He was a newly released Royal Naval Volunteer Reserve Lieutenant-Commander, and he converted her – sympathetically – into a four-berth, sea-going family cruiser.

When questioned about her unusual name, Thorpe would quietly, almost shyly, explain:

"She's named for my wife, but some who know me will tell you she is 'the other woman' in my life."

Sunset Lady was one of the so-called "little ships" – one of more than seven hundred privately owned boats that sailed from Ramsgate in England, across the Channel to Dunkirk in France, during the Second World War.

Taking part in what was known as Operation Dynamo, these small vessels – pleasure boats, private yachts and launches – were ideal for the task because they could navigate the shallow waters and get close enough to the shore to rescue the soldiers who were trapped on the beaches under enemy fire.

Between them, the "little ships" saved the lives of more than thirty thousand British and French troops.

Sunset Lady had rescued two loads of about fifty men from the beach at Dunkirk and transferred them to a destroyer lying off shore. She was damaged when alongside the destroyer the second time.

Nevertheless, Thorpe took her to the beach again, and then, fuel being low, and water seeping in due to the damage, he returned to Ramsgate where a further fifty-one men were put ashore.

The next day, after emergency repairs, he

sailed back across the Channel to the beaches, and was lucky to get back from there with still more men, even though Sunset Lady almost sank under them.

In all, so it was said, he'd lifted almost two hundred men from the beaches.

Back at Burroport, Thorpe found a bullet embedded in the front of the wheelhouse. One inch lower, and it would have come through the glass and probably into the helmsman's head.

Considering this poignant souvenir to be a lucky charm, he left it there and had it covered over with Perspex taken from the wreckage of a Spitfire which crashed near Burroport.

Initially, that is all the information I could uncover, because I never knew Thorpe himself – he died in 1948.

But, as soon as I became the legal owner of Sunset Lady, even though she was still lying sunk on the muddy bottom of Burroport harbour, I began to research her history.

My chief interest was Operation Dynamo – the Dunkirk episode. Whilst researching this I decided to become more ambitious and write up a joint biography of both James Thorpe and his Sunset Lady.

James Thorpe was born in 1890, attended grammar school, and qualified as an architect. Having started dinghy sailing as a boy, he became a keen amateur yachtsman and joined the Royal Naval Volunteer Reserve almost a year before war broke out in August 1914.

After serving in larger ships, and now a Lieutenant, he was appointed to HMS Conflict late in 1916.

Despite her name and age – Thorpe wrote in his log:

"The twenty-year-old, three-funnel destroyer 'Conflict' is a happy ship in my memory and will always remain so, especially because she introduced me to my Joyce . . ."

Chapter 2 – Thorpe's Log

It was in Spring of 1917. HMS Conflict was moored alongside the dock for boiler cleaning and minor repairs. The tide was out, so our afterdeck was only a couple of feet above the quay.

It was evening, time for the traditional naval ceremony of lowering the flag.

As Officer of the Day, I had to 'put the queen to bed' as we say.

Whilst the Petty Officer watched for a signal from a senior ship in our flotilla, my eye was caught by a very attractive young lady who stood watching us from the quayside.

The Petty Officer called, 'Sunset, sir!'

I ordered, 'Make it so!' and we both saluted as two ratings lowered and folded the White Ensign.

Immediately after the ceremony, even though

we were firmly on the mud, I found it necessary to go ashore to check our mooring lines.

The young lady asked me to explain what she had just witnessed, and – as a Naval Officer and a gentleman – I was clearly obliged to enlighten her about the significance of the sunset ceremony.

It so happened that our captain, knowing we could not sail for the next three days at least, decreed that the ward room would entertain a small number of local ladies in return for any help the townspeople gave to our ship and other visiting naval vessels.

I had little difficulty in persuading my new friend to come as my guest, though it was rather more of a problem to decide how she qualified as a 'helper'.

Then she had a brainwave. Both of her brothers were in the Navy, one commissioned, the other lower deck, and she did washing and darning when they came on leave. Said quickly, and omitting specifics, that was sufficient. My Joyce was the youngest – and by far the prettiest – of the guests.

Just before Christmas that same year we stood together on the quayside where we had first met and watched the sunset ceremony on my new ship.

The 'W' class destroyer 'Wakeful', fresh from builders on the Clyde, and only commissioned a few days earlier, looked magnificent. I sensed that Joyce shared my pride in her.

There and then I proposed to Joyce, and she accepted me. So, naturally, she has always been my 'Sunset Lady'.

The war dragged on, until we in the 'Wakeful' had the satisfaction of escorting a surrendering German Grand Fleet into Scapa Flow. Soon after that, with the war over and me due for release, I felt free to marry Joyce.

With our first child on the way, we agreed that even a well-found yacht can do too many unexpected things and is no place for a toddler, so we played it safe and bought a solid, if rather unadventurous boat, for what we both hoped would be a large family.

32-foot navy cutters are real work boats, solidly built to take hard treatment. After much heart searching, I decided on buying an unused one.

I looked for a vessel built late in the war. I knew it would probably be made from lower quality timber than one made to pre-war standards, but

I wanted a boat that hadn't suffered neglect or careless handling.

Working to my own drawings, and self-doing as much as possible, I slowly turned her into Sunset Lady – under the friendly but watchful eye of Joe Harrison, a local boat-builder.

In the bows she had a small forepeak (useful for storage), a fore cabin, a high wheelhouse with the engine room below, then a main cabin, and at the stern an open cockpit with seating. Fitted in between were the two essentials – the galley and heads.

Chapter 3 – Demoted!

In May 1940, responding to the Admiralty 'request' for privately owned powered boats of more than thirty feet, Thorpe took the 'Lady' to Sheerness in Kent, where a Royal Navy Sub-Lieutenant thanked him and gave him a travel warrant home to Burroport.

He told Thorpe that the Navy would find men to take charge of Sunset Lady.

At this Thorpe took strong exception. He made it clear that, as a Lieutenant Commander with four years of war service, he had spent the last twenty-odd years as owner and master of that vessel.

Therefore, he was far better suited than any serving Naval Officer – who 'just might happen to be available' – to take Sunset Lady to France and, equally important, to bring her back again.

Reluctantly, he was allowed to retain command, and was sent on to Ramsgate.

At Ramsgate, a Petty Officer asked him to sign a form and offered him £3 to serve for a month as a temporary ordinary seaman.

Thorpe was at first affronted, then incensed, by this suggestion.

Later, after firmly correcting the Petty Officer, he could see the funny side of it. He recalled:

More than once, in 1916, whilst serving on my biggest ship, I was threatened with demotion by an ageing, 'at-long-last-promoted' Commander named Hawkbury-Slade, still glowing under his new brass hat:

"Because, Thorpe, of your far too frequent amateur initiatives," he used to sneer.

'The Hawk', as we called him, was a little man who could, and would, stand quoting whole pages of King's regulations and Admiralty instructions whilst others did the work.

And now I am almost demoted all the way – right down to Ordinary Seaman. How old Hawkbury-Slade would love to know that!

Thorpe was given a burly, 29-year-old Able Seaman named Forster to act as signaller and crew. Since he hailed from Newcastle, he was known to one and all as Geordie.

"Ten years into my twelve," Geordie proudly announced – referring to the length of time he had signed on for when he joined up.

I recognised the type immediately. He'll scrounge, skive and drip; often in trouble, and that has kept him from being promoted. Nevertheless, sound as a bell when things really begin to happen."

Thorpe was issued with a steel helmet, provisions for three days, mainly bread and bully beef, and a large bottle of rum.

After that he supervised the refuelling of Sunset Lady. This included a number of two-gallon cans of petrol. Welcome though these were, they posed a considerable fire risk – especially when bullets might be flying.

The 'Lady' then joined the next convoy of assorted small boats and was towed across the Channel by the steam tug 'Challenge'.

Chapter 4 – The First Boat Load

En route, I had to show Forster how to deal with Sunset Lady's temperamental magneto – something no naval personnel put in charge of her would have known about.

Then, leaving him at the helm, I went below to split up the rum into several lemonade bottles and secrete these as best able, so making sure that nobody can take too much, and there will always be a generous tot for Forster and myself!

We were towed across the Channel by night, to avoid being spotted by enemy aircraft.

Before sunrise, huge clouds of black smoke are rising over the town of Dunkirk, seen silhouetted against the dawn glow and lit by fires below.

All along the coast I see flashes, though whether from guns or exploding shells, I cannot tell. But we are heading further north, to Bray Dunes, close to the Belgian border, where no sort of harbour, nor even a landing stage, awaits.

In strengthening light, I could pick out almost continuous buildings inland from the flat sand-hill coastline.

On the beach there were long lines of men, standing as though queuing for a bus.

There, we received the signal to 'cast off tow', and were left to do our best – to get as many men off, and safely on board any of the larger ships waiting well out from the shore, where there was sufficient depth of water.

I knew the maximum the Navy allowed in a 32-foot cutter like 'Lady' was forty men. But I had added a considerable amount of weight with the cabins and deck I built on to her.

Fortunately the sea is calm, and our task urgent. I told Forster that this being the first trip, we must not let more than thirty-five men come aboard.

I bring her in alongside a line of men who are up to their waists or more in the water and order Forster to drop anchor over the stern. All the men try to get on board over the same side. I yell at some to go around to the other side.

As they get on board, I order the men into the cabins, and to sit down on the floor – the lower they are, the less likely we are to capsize, as two other boats have done.

It is utter chaos. No wonder they want to get away from the beach, where, even now, bombs are exploding and bullets flying. Perhaps it is lucky that the sand is soft, so their effect is minimised, but already there are many bodies, both on shore and in the water nearby.

To make matters worse, many soldiers are still wearing steel helmets, greatcoats and even webbing equipment. It is very difficult for them to climb on board, and the sodden cloth not only weighs them down, but brings much water on board, too.

In the confusion, we lose count. I shout at Forster to haul in the anchor as I put her astern. Nothing happens until a little swell lifts her, and then we are away – to cries of dismay from the waiting men.

Chapter 5 – Dive-bombed!

I know at once, by the way she handles, that we are well overloaded.

I shout at the men to keep the pump going. The poor devils are so exhausted most of them just want to sleep – those who are not too terrified.

None were too terrified to take a swig when the rum bottle was handed round, though. Not surprisingly they left none for Forster or myself.

About a mile off shore we see several destroyers. I pick out one with the ladder down, and come alongside it. Sailors topside throw down ropes which we put around those who are too weak to climb up unaided.

I am counting, and fifty-three men leave us, five wounded in some way, though we were not able to do anything much for them.

As we turn away, back towards the noisy hell of the beach, I give the helm to Forster and go below. I gather up all the abandoned equipment and throw it overboard. I then retrieve the hidden bottle of rum.

"The sun's not yet over the yard arm," I tell Forster, "but . . . in the circumstances . . . I think we're both entitled to an Arduous Duty tot!"

Some ten minutes later I find myself wondering whether I have imbibed too freely, because I can hardly believe my eyes . . .

A narrow kayak canoe is being paddled away from the shore with soldiers astride her. We reckon that having come so far safely, they'll make it to one of the larger vessels. Having received a confident 'thumbs up' from the crazy canoeists, we leave them to it.

At the beach, we stop with water under our keel, but as men scramble on board we begin to bump on the bottom. All hell is around us. A stick of bombs falls nearby. The last one drops on the back of the line of men we are loading. I have no idea how many died in that moment.

In no time, I am forced to say that's all we can take safely this trip. I promise we will come back.

As we clear the beach, two of those pushing us off try to clamber aboard, but they are shoved back into the water. I am glad that it was done by their fellows, before I had to order them off myself.

Again, 'Lady' is very sluggish in answering the helm. I go alongside the same destroyer as before.

We have almost finished offloading our troops when another destroyer sweeps past at full speed, only concerned for her own safety. Her wash slams 'Lady' against the ladder, damaging her quite visibly.

Had 'Lady' still been full of troops, she would most probably have been swamped, dumping all fifty-six of us into the water.

The damage – all above our waterline – does not appear too serious. I am well pleased with having saved one hundred and seven men so far.

I head 'Lady' back, to honour our promise to those still on the beach.

A soldier has left his rifle on board with us. Geordie Forster fires it three times at a Stuka dive-bomber which is diving straight at us. It crashes into the sea close by. Naturally, Forster claimed this as his 'kill' and I back up his claim.

Loading has become almost routine. Now I am shouting, "Some to each side!" even before they can touch 'Lady'.

Of course, the men are frantic to get aboard, believing that it means safety. I have to make allowance for the fact that many have never set foot in a boat before.

We have a struggle to get off the beach. This time I make no promise to return, because I can see water seeping in above our normal waterline. This must be our last trip to the beach.

Chapter 6 – Two Heroes

Fuel being low, and not wishing to suffer any further damage, I make the decision to set off for Ramsgate.

I send Forster below to move more men on to the starboard side, in an attempt to raise the damage above the waterline. Again I have to urge the men to keep the pump going, bribing them with rum; though afterwards all the others got a tot, too.

Well out to sea, two bodies are seen in the water. As we approach, one waves feebly. Despite the fact that we are grossly overloaded – with more than fifty on board, and leaking too – we just cannot leave them.

I look around the boat, then shout, "This is an order: All tin hats over the side!" and, to set the example, mine is the first to go, followed by Forster's. Very reluctantly, the others follow. We have to get rid of unwanted weight.

Two soldiers – both with life jackets – are hauled on board. One is in a very bad way. The other tells me:

"Water was slopping into our boat. Those who could, were bailing frantically with their helmets. The skipper shouted, "Two with life jackets must go overboard – otherwise everybody will drown." Roddy there, leapt over the side, and – like a bloody fool – I followed him!"

Roddy died twenty minutes after he was picked up. I have no alternative but to order the men to put him back overboard.

One frightened man still has his helmet partially hidden under his greatcoat. I order the nearest man to take this from him and attach it to Roddy's ankles, to ensure he will sink and remain on the bottom.

Because word is spreading about how the two came to be in the water, there is some resentment over this, but there is no time for any pretence at a funeral. As we slip him into the water, I stand and say, loud and clear, "Greater love hath no man than this, that he did lay down his life for his friends!" It was the best I could manage, and it seemed to end the matter.

Then we hear two explosions, almost as one. Perhaps a mile away a destroyer is breaking in two and sinking. Grabbing the binoculars I can just make out her number: H88. And then she is gone – in an incredibly short time.

It is my old ship 'Wakeful'. But, heavily overloaded as we are, there is nothing we can possibly do to help.

At Ramsgate we offload 56 men. We ask for repair, but are told there is little help available. So I send Forster to 'acquire' paint and canvas to make very temporary patches inside and outside of the hull. That takes time to dry, and we need sleep, too.

That same afternoon we take on fuel and supplies. I find that two duffle coats and two blue tin hats have appeared on board. I choose not to question Forster about any of these.

Chapter 7 – Goodbye, Geordie

The time came to join the tow back to Bray Dunes on the French coast.

Whilst taking on soldiers there, a twin-engine plane, approaching from the land, fires several bursts towards us, and as it passes overhead, spent cases fall on us, but no harm is done.

Shortly after, we hear a warning shout – then we are rammed by a runaway, grey-painted ship's lifeboat. It is riddled with bullets, but still travelling at full speed, with only two dead sailors on board – obviously killed by the same plane.

Two soldiers disappear under the runaway boat as she strikes us a heavy glancing blow on the port side, ripping away a temporary patch and further damaging the planking.

The situation is now serious. "We're going, now!" I shout to Forster. "Start hauling! Now!"

Forster understands the urgency and gets a soldier to help as I set her astern. Bumping on the bottom, although only half loaded, we get clear and head out to sea.

I regret leaving men behind, but in the circumstances, we have little enough chance for ourselves and those few who are already on board.

Having got clear, I decide to offload all the soldiers onto a nearby elderly paddle steamer, but just at that moment she is hit by a bomb and begins to sink. Now it seems that the men will be as safe on our damaged 'Lady' as on a bigger ship – possibly more so.

Then I produce the rum, telling the men it will raise their spirits a little. Next, we started lightening the ship. Tin hats, webbing and – very reluctantly – greatcoats go over the side. A few rifles too, although, remembering Forster's last effort, we did keep one, fully loaded.

When well out to sea, an E-boat passes astern of 'Lady', travelling fast, but it does not fire at us.

Forster is reluctant to give them the same courtesy and gets off five rounds, though it has no visible effect.

However, two minutes later there is an explosion and the E-boat vanishes. Possibly it hit a mine, for there are plenty about, moored just beneath the surface or floating free.

Somehow, six badly wounded men are on board, and treating them uses up all our first aid equipment, but at least we are able to get to them. It would have been almost impossible if we'd taken our normal fifty plus on board.

Back at Ramsgate, we offload twenty-eight very relieved soldiers, some of whom are more than a little merry – having found the last hidden bottles of rum.

There is now no question of anybody taking 'Lady' back to France.

Again we resort to paint and canvas, and scrounge an old and 'obviously abandoned' anchor from the quayside. Forster helps me hide this on the bunk in the main cabin, to maintain an essential list to starboard to keep the damaged area out of the water.

That done, I say goodbye to the always reliable Forster, who'd been a good, loyal companion, and a great help throughout the time we'd been together.

We'd shared many dangers, and we

undoubtedly had reason to be proud that together we had saved one hundred and ninety-one men, most of whom were able to carry on the fight.

If left on the beach, many would surely have been killed or wounded, and others captured, spending the next few years as prisoners of war.

Chapter 8 – The End of the War

Now I'm going home.

The Navy is much less generous with their petrol, giving me perhaps enough to make it back to Burroport. I limp along at slow speed, always planning ahead, ready to head into the next harbour if there is a leak or the weather gets worse.

Three days later I reach Burroport with barely a gallon remaining in the tank.

The necessary repairs to her hull were beyond me, but I was able to clean her up myself, spending a lot of time scrubbing off blood stains, because I would not allow Joyce to do this.

Joe Harrison, the boat-builder, worked on 'Lady' when he could spare the time from boat-building for the Admiralty.

A few days later, when a German invasion was thought probable, orders were given that all non-essential boats must be taken up river — though just why any Germans, newly arrived by boat or parachute, would need more boats was never fully explained.

Later, with the Home Guard properly established, I managed to get 'Lady' back to Burroport again, and enrolled for coast and river patrol work.

This justified the completion of the repair work. After which, being Navy controlled, she was painted battleship grey, but I didn't get my former rank back!

Eventually, she was given a Lewis gun, which was set on a tall tripod mounted over the bow cabin. Dated 1914, it had most probably seen service throughout the Great War, and was now very temperamental.

In our practice shoots it never managed more than four consecutive shots without jamming, so we all became highly practised in the clearance drill.

Nevertheless, the one time it was fired in anger, our Lewis did excel itself with seven shots — bringing down a herring gull in the process!

But the low-flying Dornier 17 went on its way unharmed, probably unaware it had even been noticed.

To be fair, though, to our amateur gunner, the 'Flying Pencil' as it was known, was a notoriously slender target, and at some distance from our rocking boat.

For Sunset Lady the war ended on May 8th 1945, but for the Thorpe family it dragged on until September that year, when they learned that their only son, missing since the fall of Singapore, had died in a Japanese prisoner-of-war camp in 1944.

Thorpe died in 1948. His widow, Joyce, did not want to part with 'Lady', but her daughters now lived too far away to use her, and as time passed, the insurance payments lapsed.

So, she remained, swinging to her anchor, deteriorating slowly.

Chapter 9 – Call the Bomb Squad!

1956. A local newspaper headline reads:

'Mystery sinking of Dunkirk veteran – only mast tip shows at low water.'

As soon as I knew Sunset Lady had sunk, I approached both James Thorpe's widow and the harbour master. I was able to purchase the 'wreck' at a very reasonable price, within a week of her sinking.

Being well known – almost famous, locally – as an amateur diver, I also had the harbour master's permission to carry out the salvage myself.

I had been given a reasonable time in which to clear the harbour bottom. Part of the deal was that I could retain her mooring – moorings being in great demand as more boats want to come to Burroport.

My younger brother, Peter, was keen to help, but only by working from our small boat. The poor lad, being be-devilled with sinus problems, will never be able to dive with me.

I was fortunate to find a copy of The Admiralty Manual of Seamanship in the local library, and that helped me a great deal.

There was much detail on how to sling a cutter, using a multiplicity of chains when lowering it from a large warship.

However, I reckoned that with her weight under water being so much less than when suspended in air, it would be safe to lift her using only the two sling plates she was fitted with. These were both clearly shown on the diagram.

The stern sling plate was beneath the floorboards of the cockpit, so no trouble there. But Thorpe had built the fore cabin over the bow sling plate.

Because of that, I would have to drill a large hole in the cabin roof and pass our lifting rope through that. I would also need to remove the mast.

Fortunately, Mrs Thorpe found the cabin door key. I was able to dive into the wreck, open the cabin door, remove the floorboards, and find the lifting plate.

At the same time I removed as much clutter as I could, and found – to my delight –Thorpe's tin hat.

John Harrison, whose father had helped convert the 'Lady', willingly offered the use of the boatyard's pontoon – a kind of floating platform – as a lifting vessel.

By sheer good fortune we found that the pontoon was almost exactly the same length as the distance between the two sling plates, and this meant it would be easy to secure the 'Lady' underneath it.

We did calculations around the tides and worked out how, and when, to position the pontoon over the 'Lady'. When all was secure, we had to wait whilst the rising tide did its job.

So much for the theory. First I had to go down and unbolt the mast, cut that hole in the cabin roof, then enter the cabin again and pass the rope through the hole, which I hoped would help keep her upright during the recovery.

On the day, all went well. With the 'Lady' safe on the slipway, and the tide ebbing, parts of the wheelhouse became visible.

Aided by family and friends, we threw buckets of water over her, inside and out, to get rid of the mud. As soon as the water level outside the hull became lower than that inside, we began to bail her out with buckets. The hull of a boat — especially one almost thirty years old — is built to withstand external pressures, not pressures from within.

The more this water was stirred up, the more mud we got rid of. While we were still washing her out on the slipway, my brother, Peter, noticed water seeping out past something deeply embedded in the stern.

Close examination suggested possibly a 20mm cannon shell.

I knew that 20mm ammunition came in several different types. I had no hesitation in reporting our find, along with my suspicions, to the harbour master who, as usual, was indecisive.

I then went to the police, suggesting that bomb disposal experts be brought in, just in case.

At their insistence, all work on Sunset Lady stopped, and the area around the slipway was roped off. That, of course, attracted even more spectators — the very last thing we needed.

Peter remarked that had the shell struck higher up, where the timbers were thinner, it might well have gone right through and severed one of the wire cables controlling the steering gear. Then Thorpe would have been in real trouble.

A Royal Navy bomb and mine disposal team arrived in their truck with its red mudguards.

The officer in charge explained that the job had been handed to them because our 'unexploded ordnance' now lay between high and low water marks – and had come from deeper water anyway.

The team quickly confirmed that the precautions were fully justified.

Fortunately, corrosion had encouraged rot, softening the wood immediately surrounding the shell. It was almost certainly that which had caused the 'Lady' to leak, and then sink.

Having cleared everybody well away, the bomb disposal boys secured a clamp to the back end of the shell and, from a safe distance, gave a gentle pull on the attached line. Out it came. When examined it did prove to be explosive.

I was disappointed, because it meant I was not allowed to keep it as part of Sunset Lady's history.

However, the bomb disposal boys did very

kindly send me the next best thing – an identical, fired, inert 20mm shell. They also provided me with a whole, but deactivated German round with its brass case. These are now displayed on board.

Around the time when she was struck by the shell, the 'Lady' would probably have been hitting floating or submerged objects, so even such a heavy impact at the stern would not have been noticed as anything exceptional.

Being only 20mm, it must have come from an aircraft attack, because the Germans were, at that time, still some distance from the beach, so no shells of this small size could have come from the land.

Chapter 10 – Back Afloat

After raising the 'Lady', I was surprised at the complexity of sprockets, chains, wires and pulleys Thorpe and Harrison devised to enable the rudders to be operated remotely from the wheelhouse, forward and reverse.

Originally, the rudder would have been worked by a helmsman, who steered standing at the stern with his hand on a conventional tiller.

When Sunset Lady was safely back afloat, I visited Mrs Thorpe and explained what I was intending to do. She told me what little she knew, but Thorpe had been unwilling to talk about his part in the evacuation.

Three days later I was invited to visit her again. To my joy she had found the diary Thorpe kept during his time at Dunkirk.

In fact it was a log book, to which he had added

a whole lot of very interesting detail, almost certainly after getting home.

Mrs Thorpe entrusted this somewhat battered book to me, with firm instructions that if I ever sold the 'Lady', this paperwork was to go with her, or to the National Maritime Museum, whichever I thought more appropriate at the time.

Now, we set about reconditioning the 'Lady', as close to her appearance at Dunkirk as possible.

At one stage though, halfway through the laborious task of scraping away the grey paint, I found myself regretting that decision. But when she was resplendent with her newly applied varnish, we could take a real pride in her.

I installed a large press photograph of James Thorpe. This was taken immediately after he returned her to Burroport, and in it he clearly shows the strain of his gallant action.

When Mrs Thorpe saw that I really was carrying out my promise to restore Sunset Lady as a tribute to her husband and the men he brought back, she further entrusted me with Thorpe's private diaries from World War One – on the strict condition that I only quote from the naval entries, and did not disclose the very personal material referring to herself. And I have always scrupulously respected her trust.

In 1966 I learned that a commemorative plaque:

Dunkirk
1940

could be worn by all surviving veteran Dunkirk boats. I put in my claim for Sunset Lady, and was accepted as a full member of the Association of Dunkirk Little Ships. Thus, she became officially recognised and honoured as one of the "Little Ships of Dunkirk".

I proudly attached her plaque to the front of the wheelhouse, beside the German bullet, and invited Mrs Thorpe to come down and unveil it in front of the local press photographer.

This led to more publicity, local and national. As a result, Geordie Forster, and three of the men who had been saved by Thorpe and Sunset Lady contacted me.

Later I was pleased to install a 1940s photo of Geordie Forster in his uniform, beside the picture of Thorpe.

I asked the local newspaper to help organise a reunion of those saved by the pair of them, and of course I made a point of writing down all their stories. These are now kept safe, together with Thorpe's diary and log book.

Chapter 11 – Getting Answers

There was still one part of my story largely unexplained.

Forster – being a Geordie – remembered that the two men picked up mid-Channel were both in the North Riding Regiment, and this at least was a starting point for further investigations.

But time and again I came up against a brick wall. After being asked, "Are you next of kin?" or "Do you have the consent of next of kin?" I was unable to proceed any further.

The next best thing, I thought, would be the local press, and learning that the North Riding Regimental Depot was at Claxtenby, I wrote a long letter to the editor of the Claxtenby Clarion.

I had it all finished, addressed, sealed and stamped, when an entirely different approach came to mind.

I recalled somebody saying, "Rank can usually sidestep regulation," so I decided to put that to the test. I started another, far more deferential letter, and posted that alone.

Ten days later I received a reply – in an impressive envelope.

The Colonel-in-Chief of the North Riding Regiment graciously assured me that I had her support, and could now expect full co-operation from both the Army Records Office and the North Riding's Regimental Archives – the letter being signed by the royal lady herself.

I wrote to the North Riding's Archive, asking to visit, and they gave me an appointment.

I gave the archivist all the information I had.

"Roddy?" asked the archivist. "Probably a private? Is that all you can tell me?"

It wasn't much to go on.

"And it's probably a nickname . . ." he mused. But then he remembered something and began rummaging among his folders.

"There is a local family, named Rodderik," he told me. "Three sons – all from the North Riding

Regiment – were lost in the war. Let me show you."

He produced a sheaf of papers.

"The oldest, Roderick Rodderik, he is listed as 'missing' around your Dunkirk time. The others died in Tobruk and at Monte Casino . . . they certainly got into the thick of it. Who else was it survived on your boat?"

"Burrows," I told him. "I can remember that, because I come from Burroport."

The archivist dug into his files again.

"Now, let's see. Oh, he's recorded as dying in an air raid in London, June 4th 1940. That suggests he never got back to his family, so they'd know nothing of his action before being picked up by your boat. It's probable they got nothing but a postcard saying he was safe and back in England."

He turned over more pages before asking, "Do you know of the Riding's Book of Remembrance in the abbey? One page of it is turned every day. Now if your 'Roddy' turns out to be Roderick Rodderik, the book will have to be updated.

"I expect it is now too late to get some official recognition for the two men who nobly chose to go overboard, as they did, but the fact deserves to be recorded in some way – possibly in that book, when the detail of Rodderik's death is added.

"That is just possible, because I know corrections and additions have been made in the past."

Chapter 12 – Still Loved

The ageing Sunset Lady is our family boat, but whenever possible I take her to the "Little Ship" rallies, and, escorted by the Royal Navy, we have taken her back to Dunkirk, where we were welcomed by the townspeople.

On that trip, as on other major occasions, we exercised our right to wear the St George's Cross at our bow – a privilege granted by the Admiralty, and normally reserved for themselves. Though, at the same time, we had to wear the Red Ensign at the stern, just in case anyone might think we were acting above our station.

Sunset Lady has also attended other wartime commemorations, always proudly wearing the House Flag of the Association of Dunkirk Little Ships at the masthead. That is the red-on-white Saint George's Cross, defaced in the centre with the arms of the City of Dunquerque.

These flags and privileges, of course, belong first and foremost to the vessel, rather than the current owner, who, in some cases, had not even been born when the boat had her finest hour.

We always welcome visitors on board, and in so doing the 'Lady' has helped to raise money for various service charities.

James Thorpe would doubtless be glad to know that his Sunset Lady is still loved, respected, and well maintained.

I am sure he would be equally happy to know that his grandson, and twelve-year-old great-grandson, were on board as crew when the 'Lady' joined other "Little Ships" at Ramsgate for the 70th anniversary cruise to Dunkirk at the end of May 2010.

CPSIA information can be obtained
at www.ICGtesting.com
Printed in the USA
LVHW111058060120
642635LV00001B/159/P